WILD PARSNIP:
THE WEED THAT
BURNS, BLISTERS AND SCARS

A Landowner's Battle Against the
Aggressive Invader

By C. Poole

Dedicated to all the private land owners that enjoy the meadows and the ground nesting birds. May you read, be warned and defend your land from the Wild Parsnip invasion

Disclaimer

This book is believed to contain accurate information based on my personal study of the literature available. The references are provided for the reader's further research efforts. I do not make any warranty, express or implied or assume any legal responsibility for the accuracy, completeness, or usefulness of any information. The information in this book should not be a substitute for professional advice and training.

The author does not have any professional training in botany or weed management, but only personal experience and reading to defend the land from this weed invader. The author recommends that readers contact their State natural resource authorities for more information.

Table of Contents

Chapter One

The Invasion and Discovery   6

Chapter Two

What Makes Wild Parsnip So
Dangerous   10

Protection From
Furocoumarin in the Wild   17

Chapter Three

Why I Can't Control the Wild
Parsnip Invasion   20

Chapter Four

Noxious or Invasive?   30

Chapter Five

Details and Recognition of
The Invader   33

My Home Grown
Attempts to Reduce
the Invasion   37

Index   42

Chapter One
The Invasion and Discovery

I have been fighting a battle against Wild Parsnip on 40 acres in southwest Wisconsin for the past decade. I purchased a beautiful meadowland on a ridge-top with grasses, milkweed, and oats 13 years ago. Within a year of buying the land, two of my neighbors with acreage west of my property told me of a burning rash and blistering that prompted them to see a physician. The physicians were unable to recognize the cause, but a park ranger could. It was Wild Parsnip and it was growing on their land.

At the time they were diagnosed independently, my neighbors and I observed no Wild Parsnip on my 40 acres. I knew what the adult weed looked like from natural resource department literature, but not the immature growth. Within two years, I had a large number of flowered, mature Wild Parsnip plants in my field.

The challenge of defeating this major invader continues to this day.

This book is intended to share my personal study and experience with those who have not yet had the unfortunate exposure and motivation to study this aggressive and dangerous weed.

It is my hope that reading my experience will prevent others from the failed trials and health risks that I encountered trying to eliminate the weed.

It is the toxic juice, or sap, within the plant that makes this weed so dangerous. Wild Parsnip produces furocoumarins, a secondary plant metabolite in the sap. The toxic furocoumarin is no accident of nature. It is intended to chemically damage the cells of the predators of the plant, including mammals.

Natural resource authorities often state that you must break a leaf or stem to be exposed to the toxin. I have pictures and experience to demonstrate that the plant exudes the toxin on the leaves and stems, possibly after insect attack. The plant produces copious amounts of sap. Simply touching the sap on the plant will expose the skin to the toxic chemical. No one is immune to the effect.

Mowing, trimming or pulling the plant increases the risk and anecdotal emergency room reports are full of trimming exposures. The skin damage is sometimes misdiagnosed as herbicide exposure or poison ivy when the victim reports landscaping work.

The furocoumarin causes a phytophoto-dermatitis. The plant toxin requires exposure to ultraviolet-A light to initiate the skin cell destruction. Even a cloudy day will provide sufficient light to cause skin damage. In a later chapter I will describe in detail the furocoumarin action.

During my regional travel to neighboring States, I have observed Wild Parsnip in road ditches and along rail road tracks. In horror, I have observed pedestrians and bikers pass by those weeds without recognition. I have had the opportunity to discuss the weed with two friends who are master gardeners in two neighboring States, neither who had any awareness of Wild Parsnip dangers.

As a veteran of the constant potential exposure to the toxin and the pervasive and nearly indestructible nature of the enemy weed, it is hard to believe I didn't know what it looked like a decade ago. Now, I can recognize it in all stages and from a safe distance. I hope my story is helpful to you.

Chapter Two

What Makes Wild Parsnip So Dangerous?

Skin exposure to the juice of the weed, activated by sunlight, even on a cloudy day, causes a burning erythema (red rash) after a day or two following exposure.   It does not itch. No one is immune to the toxin.

Phytophotodermatitis was discovered in 1942 and led to photomedicine. Photomedicine uses the plant toxins and light in controlled settings to destroy selected skin cells. The plant toxin is referred to as psoralen in clinical trials. Based on my reading, this is the type of furocoumarin in Wild Parsnip.

Wild Parsnip plant toxins combine with the victim's DNA and destroy epithelial cells in the skin. This is no controlled setting, and the dose is variable. The plant produces more of the chemical after injury and during flowering. It is intended as a defense mechanism against predators.

Unfortunately, the weed is juicy. Accidental exposure is possible by simply walking near the plant. Sometimes I observe the sap dripping down the outside of the stalk. This may be due to an insect attack, but it still contains the plant juice.

A casual hiker could brush against the weed and think they had a burn injury the following day. The scars will take the shape of the physical sap contact, as drops, spots, streaks, or drips.

Hand prints, by indirect exposure from an adult victim of Wild Parsnip juice on the skin of children have been misdiagnosed as child abuse. Exposure after trimming or mowing is especially serious, because the plant tissue and toxic sap is pulverized and widely sprayed.

Picture 1 Wild Parsnip leaf with obvious sap in mid June.

After the burning erythema (rash), depending on the degree of exposure and the toxicity of the juice, a bullous eruption (blister) will appear. After a few days, the blister should subside, if it is not infected.

Over a decade ago, local physicians could not identify the exposure of Wild Parsnip in my neighbors. Currently, in our region, physicians are familiar with the symptoms and the cause. I suspect that in non-endemic, but emerging invasion regions, victims and physicians do not know the cause of the injury.

There are anecdotal reports in dermatology journals, but it is unlikely a medical practitioner may recognize the Wild Parsnip exposure until it is epidemic in the community.

The red and sometimes odd shaped contact rash, burns, but does not itch. The blister (bullous eruption) is large and subject to breaking and infection. The post-inflammatory response leads to cell necrosis (death) and scarring for months.

The extreme Wild Parsnip skin damage has been reportedly misdiagnosed as child abuse, cancer, blood disorders, impetigo, fungal infections, and poison ivy.

The erythema and eruptions are not an immune response, as in Poison Ivy. It is caused by the actual DNA destruction of the epithelial cells by the furocoumarins in the plant.

No one is immune to Wild Parsnip. It is not caused by allergy. There is no treatment except for symptoms. Cold compresses, analgesics and topical steroids are used to relieve symptoms.

Without the addition of ultraviolet light, the furocoumarins are weakly mutagenic (cause genetic mutations). With ultraviolet A light, the furocoumarins are genotoxic (damages DNA) and mutagenic to bacteria and yeasts by binding the DNA. [1]

Topical (skin) application in mice caused papillomas and carcinomas of the squamous epithelium[2].

Other plants contain furocoumarins. Parsnips, celery, lime oil and bergamot oil had the highest quantity of furocoumarins based on studies. Grapefruit measures 2-10 mg/kg and limes 300-500[3]. Lime juice

[1] Eisenbrand, Dr. G, "Toxicological Assessment of Furocoumarins in Foodstuffs", 2004 Senate Commission on Food Safety, Germany, p 12 www.dfg.de/download/pdf/dfg_im_profit/reden_stellungnahmen/2006/sklm_furocoum arine_en_2006.pdf

[2] Eisenbrand, Dr. G., "Toxicological Assessment..", p 10

[3] Eisenbrand, Dr. G., "Toxicological Assessment..", p3

sometimes causes a burning rash in bartenders.

Cultivated parsnips measured 3 mg/kg, but microbial infected parsnips in storage reached a concentration of 2500 mg/kg[4]. I suspect it is likely that wild parsnips are even more likely to be microbially infested. The plant produces increased furocoumarins when injured or infected.

Oral toxicity of furocoumarins have been studied in animals. Adenomas and adenocarcinomas of the kidney in male rats occurred at 37 and 75 mg/kg, even without added UVA light exposure[5].

Furocoumarins used as phototherapy in medicine has provided data for human safety evaluations. 1300 psoriasis patients were treated with 500-600 micrograms furocoumarins/kg body weight and UVA light to target abnormal skin cells. In studies

[4] Eisenbrand, Professor G., "Toxicological Assessment of Furocoumarins in Foodstuffs", Kaiserslautern University of Technology, Germany, Senate Commission on Food Safety, September 22, 2006 p 3
www.dfg.de/download/pdf/dfg_im_profit/reden_stellungnahmen/2006/sklm_furocoum arine_en_2006.pdf

www.dfg.de/download/pdf/dfg_im_profit/reden_stellungnahmen/2006/sklm_furocoum arine_en_2006.pdf

[5] Eisenbrand, Dr. G., "Toxicological Assessment of Furocoumarins in Foodstuffs", 2004 Senate Commission on Food Safety p 10-11

following the patients, there was a dose dependent increase in squamous epithelium carcinomas[6], basal cell carcinomas[7] and melanomas[8]. Of 892 men in the group, there was a dose dependent increase in genital tumors[9]. In 1999, another study confirmed the increased risk of cutaneous squamous cell carcinoma, but not malignant melanoma.[10]

I am not concerned about cancer risk from exposure to the Wild Parsnip. Some of the studies were based on oral dosing and

[6] Eisenbrand, Dr. G, "Toxicological Assessment of Furocoumarins in Foodstuffs", 2004 Senate Commission on Food Safety, Germany, p 13 Stern, R.S. Liebman, EJ, Vakeva, L, (1998) Oral Psoralen and Ultraviolet A Light (PUVA) Treatment of Psoriasis and Persistent Risk of Non Melanoma Skin Cancer, Journal of the National Cancer Institute, 90, 1278-1284

[7] Eisenbrand, Dr. G, "Toxicological Assessment of Furocoumarins in Foodstuffs", 2004 Senate Commission on Food Safety, Germany, p 13 referencing Katz, KA, Marcil, I, Stern, R S., (2002) Incidence and Risk Factors Associated with a Second Squamous Cell Carcinoma or Basal Cell Carcinoma in Psoralen and Ultraviolet A Light Treated Psoriasis Patients, Journal of Investigative Dermatology, 118 (6) 1038-1043

[8] Eisenbrand, Dr. G, "Toxicological Assessment of Furocoumarins in Foodstuffs", 2004 Senate Commission on Food Safety, Germany, p 13-14 referencing Stern, R. S., et al (2001) The Risk of Melanoma in Association with Long Term Exposure to PUVA, Journal of American Academy of Dermatology, 44, 755-761

[9] Eisenbrand, Dr. G, "Toxicological Assessment of Furocoumarins in Foodstuffs", 2004 Senate Commission on Food Safety, Germany, p 13-14 referencing Stern, R.S., Bagheri, S., Nicholsk, et al (2002) The Persistent Risk of Genital Tumors Among Men Treated With Psoralen Plus Ultraviolet A (PUVA) for Psoriasis Journal American Academy of Dermatology 47 33-39

[10] Lindelof, B, Sigurgeirsson, B, Tegner, E., British Journal of Dermatology, 1999 141: 108-112 http://onlinelibrary.wiley.com/doi/10.1046/j.1365-2133.1999.02928.x

treatment 100-200 times. Few victims of accidental exposure would subject themselves more than a few times. I include this information to show the potential damage of this plant toxin.

The review of the furocoumarin toxicity literature was presented to the German Senate Commission on Food Safety in 2004 to evaluate the presence of plant chemicals in food.

Protection From Furocoumarin Exposure in the Wild

Is there a way to avoid the erythema? Until recently, I thought if I washed thoroughly after working in the field I would avoid the skin damage. However, a dedicated Wisconsin naturalist conducted a skin test to measure the effect of washing the skin after exposure to Wild Parsnip juice. He found that washing just 10 minutes after the skin exposure was not adequate to avoid the reaction. [11]

---

[11] Eagan, David J, "Wild Parsnip II", Wisconsin Department of Natural Resources Magazine, June 2000, dnr.wi.gov/wnrmag/html/stories/2000/jun00parsnip.htm

Natural resource authorities suggest wearing long sleeves, long pants and gloves when working around Wild Parsnip. Based on the accidental exposure of eyes and hands of friends, I would add safety glasses and chemically resistant long gloves that cover the wrists and upper arms. Standard garden gloves can absorb the juice and lead to exposure. The work clothes should be removed and washed after any work near the plant.

Natural resource authorities warn against using motorized trimmers because they pulverize the weed and juice. The option of hand trimming may also create skin and face exposure as gardeners lean down toward the weed.

Some natural resource authorities recommend working the weeds later in the evening to avoid the sunlight exposure and then shower immediately. The chemical activation of the furocoumarins by sunlight is most pronounced in the first two hours after exposure. The chemical is still potentially dangerous after this period.

Example Wild Parsnip in bloom

Chapter Three
Why I Can't Control the Wild Parsnip Invasion

The weed and its toxic juice are dangerous to humans and to animals. The weed obviously must die. However, the weed is proliferating in my region of the country. Not only has it spread quickly on my property, but it has been almost impossible to destroy. The following is a description of the recommendations for control and my personal experience.

Initially, when I recognized the weed, I presumed I could burn it out. However, I read the weed is extremely hardy after fires and re-sprouts before the other weed competitors. It has a deep tap root, allowing it to survive and flourish following fires.

Natural resource authorities suggest following a burn with application of an herbicide on the new re-sprouted growth. I have tried application of herbicide and killed only the leaves where I applied the chemical, instead of the entire plant. I have applied two large hand pump tanks of a recommended herbicide directly on the Wild Parsnip plants in my field with little result. There was recent testimony to a U.S. House Subcommittee that included an illustration of Wild Parsnip and other weeds that increased in abundance in glyphosate-resistant crops in Iowa. [12].

Natural resource authorities suggest digging out the plant an inch or two below the surface with a shovel. The shear numbers of weeds on my property logistically prevents digging out individual plants.

My Wild Parsnip experience has been that the plant re-grows quickly. I choose to dig out the entire root in newly invaded areas. The root is deep and sometimes thick, so large holes are created in extraction. The plant must be grasped to pull it out of the ground and my gloves got wet with the juice of the plant. Another concern was that by

[12] Owen, Dr. Michael, PhD, "Herbicide Resistant Weeds In Genetically Engineered Crops", U.S. House Domestic Policy Subcommittee, House Committee on Oversight and Government Reform, "Are Superweeds an Outgrowth of USDA Biotech Policy", July 28, 2010 http://oversight.house.gov/index. 921:07-28-2010-domestic-policy-qare-20100728Owen.pdf

reaching toward the ground I was exposing my face and eyes to accidental spray of the juicy plant.

Picture 2 A root and stalk of Wild Parsnip that was dug out two days earlier in mid June It is about 14 inches total length.

A century ago, the parsnip webworm was discovered and controlled the weed. The potential increase in the plant toxicity as a result of exposure to webworms is theorized. Parsnip webworms recently and quickly infested Wild Parsnip in New Zealand that had not been previously exposed to the webworm.[13] The webworms may still be

[13] Zangerl, A.R., M.C. Stanley, M.R. Berenbaum, "Selection for Chemical Trait Remixing in an Invasive Weed After Reassociation with a Co-evolved Specialist", Proceedings of the National Academy of Sciences of the U.S. 2008. March 25, 105 (12) 4547 www.pnas.org/cgi/content/full/0710280105/DC1

useful for a small invasion, but are ineffective for a large problem area because of higher toxicity of the plant in the U.S. I have observed ants eating the seeds of the weed on my property. However, I believe there are far too many weeds and too few ants on the planet for my weed.

Regular mowing is recommended by most authorities to keep the plant from flowering. Early in the season, the rosettes are close to the ground and unaffected by the mower. On my property, the mowed plants produce shorter shoots and flowers that sprout between mowing cycles. The leaves re-grow within days of mowing.

Constant mowing at intervals to prevent the plant from an opportunity to flower may be the most effective option for large properties with large numbers of plants like mine. Regular mowing has worked well for a neighbor who has large mowing equipment and after ten years of regular mowing does not have obvious Wild Parsnip.

Picture 3 Re-growth of Wild Parsnip leaf only 5 days after mowing.

Recent road maintenance policies in several States require the first mowing be delayed until after July 15 for cost control and to allow bird hatching. These policies encourage the Wild Parsnip seeding. Authorities have reported that mowing after the seeds are formed can easily spread the wild parsnip seeds locally and also reduce the vigor of competitive species.   Iowa recently passed a law prohibiting road crews and private landowners from mowing the right of way until late in the season. Iowa has also recently announced a Wild Parsnip invasion.

Picture 4 Mature Wild Parsnip plant mid-July

Picture 5 Mature Wild Parsnip plant with seeds mid August

According to authorities, Wild Parsnip invades disturbed soil, but not healthy prairies. However, my property and my adjoining neighbor's property was invaded without disturbed soil. The parsnip came from the west.

The only existing patch of parsnip is a half mile west of the property along a State and county highway ditch below our ridge properties.

Within two years of the adjoining properties invasion, my property was similarly invaded beginning from the west and moving towards the east in a swath that progresses about fifty feet a year.

According to authorities, the seeds disperse within ten foot of the mother plant, but the spread on my property is five times farther each year. Currently, the invasion has almost reached the eastern edge, and will no doubt invade the valley below our property in the next few years.

Picture 6 Close-up of Wild Parsnip mature plant with seeds

I have tried other novel approaches to reduce the weed. Knowing that it likes the sun, I have planted tree seedlings to produce shade. Where I have a volunteer ash tree, sumac or bush, I encourage its growth.

In an attempt to create competition, I have plowed areas of Wild Parsnip invasion, torn the roots with the plow, and planted Buckwheat seeds. The laughable response of the Wild Parsnip is displayed in Picture 7.

Picture 7 Wild Parsnip root plowed a week earlier re-grows leaves on damaged root

Chapter Four
Noxious or Invasive?

It is aggressive, toxic, and extremely hardy. Unfortunately, it is generally not treated as a noxious weed and there is no recognition of the potential invasive encouragement in road mowing policies.

The weed is invading more new territories of the U.S. and those populations are unfamiliar with the weed or the exposure risks. Land owners cannot control the weed if they don't recognize it. Pictures are usually available of the mature plant, but not the immature plant. By the time I recognized the immature weed, it was already out of control.

Natural resource authorities in most states have information available, if the landowners know the name of the plant. I have observed colorful brochures and signs posted about the Garlic Mustard weed in Wisconsin, but not Wild Parsnip. Garlic

Mustard is considered an alien species, but Wild Parsnip is considered naturalized since the 1890's.

Wild Parsnip is only considered a noxious weed in one State, Ohio, according to official lists. It is considered invasive in Michigan, Pennsylvania, Tennessee, Virginia, and Wisconsin.[14] Minnesota currently lists Wild Parsnip on their state controlled list of noxious weeds.[15] Iowa issued a warning about the invasive species in 2007. The U.S. Forestry Service does not include it on the list of noxious weeds. However, it is considered invasive in two national parks, Yellowstone and Colonial National Historical Park in Virginia.

I found a Wild Parsnip assessment by a noxious weed committee in Colorado surprising. They considered the overall ecological impact of the weed to be mild. They considered the weed not especially dominant, but merely very competitive. The report repeated the assertion of other natural resources authorities that prairies tend to be

[14] U.S. Forest Service, Invasive Plants http://www.na.fs.fed.us/fhp/invasive_plants

[15] Minnesota Department of Agriculture, Minnesota Noxious Weed www.mda.state.mn.us/plants/badplants/noxiouslist.aspx

resistant to invasion. They believed the local rate of spread, was likely to be limited, due to the species restricted sexual reproduction[16]. These findings are similar to other state and federal government reports.

It is the frequent official position, but not my private landowner experience. My land was not disturbed, but a meadow, already dense with grass and oats. The Wild Parsnip quickly infiltrated and reproduced wildly.

[16] Colorado Noxious Weed Advisory Committee, "Criteria for Categorizing Invasive Non-native Plants That Threaten Colorado's Wildland and Agriculture", December 4 2008 www.colorado.gov/agconservation/psativa.pdf

Chapter Five

Details and Recognition of Wild Parsnip

Wild Parsnip is Pastinaca Sativa. It originated in Eurasia. It is the wild variety of the cultivated parsnip plant. The weed lives for two years. It initially produces a leafy rosette close to the ground. The rosette must achieve a minimum size to support the flower production.

Picture 8 Example of rosette appearing in April and May

Picture 9 New leaf growing from mowed stalk. Mowed 4 days before picture of re-growth.

If the rosette is cut or burned, it re-sprouts again from the deep tap root.

I have observed that instead of several leaves, there are one or two leaves that re-sprout and grow quickly upward after mowing.

The rosette weed produces a tall shoot with a greenish yellow flower resembling Queen Anne's Lace in mid summer. In June, the flower is bright green. Natural resources authorities call the bloom yellow, but it is an ugly greenish yellow in my opinion. It has wide elliptical leaves that resemble carrot leaves but are hairy on both sides. The plant is described as mucilaginous.

Picture 10 Obvious sap dripping from leaf mid June

The 1000 seeds of the plant mature in June or July and are distributed through September. The seeds supposedly disperse within 10 foot of the plant. My personal opinion based on the west to east progression on my property is that wind distributes the seed effectively. The weed stands above the other weeds in the field. The seeds of Wild Parsnip are hardy. They can survive four years on the ground and germinate when the conditions are right.

Picture 11 Mature plant with seeds

The plant grows well in drought conditions and after burning because of the deep tap root and reduced competition.

My Home Grown Attempts to Reduce the Invasion

The weed loves the sun so I have planted trees to increase shade. This has not been a limited endeavor. I have planted 1000, three year old cedar and spruce seedlings.

I have plowed a section of the property, particularly invaded by the parsnip, and seeded clover, chicory and buckwheat.

In the fall season, I have tried to collect stems with seeds still attached, and burn them. I succeeded in creating a Wild Parsnip invasion around the fire pit!

I would recommend that if there are fewer than a thousand plants, take the time to dig them up using a shovel, but use face and hand protection. I wish I had taken this action. They should be dug out early in the season to avoid accidental seeding.

If you have more than a thousand plants, create shade, create competition and plow or mow for several years to eliminate the plant. These are my personal recommendations based on my experience with this weed.

When successful methods are found, they will take years to eliminate most of the weeds. The plant takes two years to complete the life cycle. The seeds could survive another four years. It is possible to eliminate the invasion on a carefully managed property in six years.

Since the Wild Parsnip invasion, I have no longer created hiking trails and bird nesting boxes in the middle of the field because of the risk of exposure.

My efforts have all been directed at battling the Wild Parsnip. I even welcome the occasional sighting of thistle and dandelion. Nothing is as bad as the Wild Parsnip to me.

The Wild Parsnip prevents me from enjoying the property because from May to August I am at risk of exposure to the sap.

I do not want to mow the field on a continuous basis because of the high population of ground nesting birds.

I have found herbicides ineffective and prefer not to use chemicals in the hope to produce an organic crop in the future.

I wish I had been more aware of the risk and identification of the immature plant before the invasion. I would have dug up the immature plants.

My recommendation is for all property owners of land in the 46 affected States, to monitor the flowers of weeds in June or July for the presence of Wild Parsnip. A cursory look for a Queen Ann's Lace-appearing plant with a greenish-yellow flower should be further evaluated for confirmation. Road ditches and rail road right of ways are invasion patterns of this weed.

Support State natural resources authorities in Wild Parsnip control efforts. Those efforts must apply equally to government property and road maintenance policies, in addition to private landowners.

Primarily, I hope that this book has been useful to readers in identifying the immature and mature plant and recognizing the invasion risk, before it is too late.

I hope that you can enjoy your meadow and avoid the battle that I have endured. I encourage all readers to share the information in this book and to further study this menace.

Picture 12 Wild Parsnip with seeds in August

INDEX and SUGGESTED READING

Cather, Jennifer Clay, Mark Macknet, M Alan Menter, "Hyperpigmented Macules and Streaks", Proceedings Baylor University medical Center, 2000 October 13 (4) 405-406

www.baylorhealth.edu/proceedings/13_4/13_4_cather.htm/

Colorado Noxious Weed Advisory Committee, "Criteria for Categorizing Invasive Non-native Plants That Threaten Colorado's Wildland and Agriculture", December 4 2008
www.colorado.gov/agconservation/psativa.pdf

Eagan, David J, "Wild Parsnip II", Wisconsin Department of Natural Resources Magazine, June 2000, dnr.wi.gov/wnrmag

Eisenbrand, Dr. G, "Toxicological Assessment of Furocoumarins in Foodstuffs", 2004 Senate Commission on Food Safety, Germany, p 12
www.dfg/de/download/pdf.../sklm_furocoumarinee_en_2006.pdf

EDDMapS, Early Dectection and Distribution Mapping System, Center for Invasive Species and Ecosystem Health, www.invasiveplantatlas.org

Eisenbrand, Professor G., "Toxicological Assessment of Furocoumarins in Foodstuffs", Kaiserslautern University of Technology, Germany, Senate Commission on Food Safety, September 22, 2006 p 3
www.dfg.de/download/pdf/dfg_im_profit/reden_stellungnahmen/2006/sklm_furocoumarine_en_2006.pdf

Hill, P.F., M. Pickford, N.Parkhouse, "Phytophotodermatitis Mimicking Child Abuse", Jrnal of the Royal Society of Medicine, Vol.90 October 1997, 560-561,
www.ncbi.nlm.nih.gov/pmc/articles/PMC1296598

Iowa Integrated Crop Management, "Weed Watch Wild Parsnip and Poison Hemlock", www.ipm.iastate.ed/ipm/icm/node/2549/print

Katz, KA, Marcil, I Stern, R S., (2002) Incidence and Risk Factors Associated with a Second Squamous Cell Carcinoma or Basal Cell Carcinoma in Psoralen and Ultraviolet A Light Treated Psoriasis Patients, Journal of Investigative Dermatology, 118 (6) 1038-1043 referenced in Eisenbrand, Dr. G, "Toxicological Assessment of Furocoumarins in Foodstuffs", 2004 Senate Commission on Food Safety, Germany, p 13

Lindelof, B, Sigurgeirsson, B, Tegner, E., "Phytophotodermatitis Associated with Parsnip Picking", British Journal of Dermatology, 1999 141: 108-112 http://onlinelibrary.wiley.com/doi/10.1046/j.11365-2133.1999.02928x

Minnesota Department of Agriculture, Minnesota Noxious Weed www.mda.state.mn.us/plants/badplants/noxiouslist.aspx

Owen, Dr. Michael, PhD, "Herbicide Resistant Weeds In Genetically Engineered Crops", U.S. House Domestic Policy Subcommittee, House Committee on Oversight and Government Reform, "Are Superweeds an Outgrowth of USDA Biotech Policy", July 28, 2010 http://oversight.house.gov/index. 20100728Owen.pdf Table 2

Shepherd, Suzanne Moore, MD, "Plant Poisoning, Phytophototoxins" emedicine.medscape.com

Stern, R.S. Liebman, EJ, Vakeva, L, (1998) Oral Psoralen and Ultraviolet A Light (PUVA) Treatment of Psoriasis and Persistent Risk of Non Melanoma Skin Cancer, Journal of the National Cancer Institute, 90, 1278-1284 referenced in Eisenbrand, Dr. G, "Toxicological Assessment of Furocoumarins in Foodstuffs", 2004 Senate Commission on Food Safety, Germany, p 13

Stern, R. S., et al (2001) The Risk of Melanoma in Asssociation with Long Term Exposure to PUVA, Journal of American Academy of Dermatology, 44, 755-761 referenced in Eisenbrand, Dr. G,

"Toxicological Assessment of Furocoumarins in Foodstuffs", 2004 Senate Commission on Food Safety, Germany, p 13-14

Stern, R.S., Bagheri, S., Nicholsk, et al (2002) The Persistent Risk of Genital Tumors Among Men Treated With Psoralen Plus Ultraviolet A (PUVA) for Psoriasis Journal American Academy of Dermatology 47 33-39 referenced in Eisenbrand, Dr. G, "Toxicological Assessment of Furocoumarins in Foodstuffs", 2004 Senate Commission on Food Safety, Germany, p 13-14

U.S. Forest Service, Invasive Plants
http://www.na.fs.fed.us/fhp/invasive_plants

Wisconsin Department of Natural Resources, "Wild Parsnip", http://dnr.wi.gov/invasives/fact/parsnip.htm

Zangerl, A.R., M.C. Stanley, M.R. Berenbaum, "Selection for Chemical Trait Remixing in an Invasive Weed After Reassociation with a Co-evolved Specialist", Proceedings of the National Academy of Sciences of the U.S. 2008. March 25, 105 (12) 4547, www.pnas.org/cgi/content/full/0710280105/DC1

All pictures by author

www.ingramcontent.com/pod-product-compliance
Lightning Source LLC
Chambersburg PA
CBHW070237290526
45789CB00004B/1661